THE LITTLE BOOK OF

IRISH
BLESSINGS

Published in 2024 by OH!
An Imprint of Welbeck Non-Fiction Limited,
part of Welbeck Publishing Group.
Offices in: London – 20 Mortimer Street, London W1T 3JW
and Sydney – Level 17, 207 Kent St, Sydney NSW 2000 Australia
www.welbeckpublishing.com

Compilation text © Welbeck Non-Fiction Limited 2023
Design © Welbeck Non-Fiction Limited 2023

Disclaimer:
This book and the information contained herein are for general educational
and entertainment use only. The contents are not claimed to be exhaustive,
and the book is sold on the understanding that neither the publishers nor the
author are thereby engaged in rendering any kind of professional services.
Users are encouraged to confirm the information contained herein with other
sources and review the information carefully with their appropriate, qualified
service providers. Neither the publishers nor the author shall have any
responsibility to any person or entity regarding any loss or damage whatsoever,
direct or indirect, consequential, special or exemplary, caused or alleged to be
caused, by the use or misuse of information contained in this book.

All rights reserved. No part of this publication may be reproduced, stored
in a retrieval system, or transmitted in any form or by any means (including
electronic, mechanical, photocopying, recording, or otherwise) without prior
written permission from the publisher.

ISBN 978-1-80069-555-9

Compiled and written by: Malcolm Croft
Editorial: Victoria Denne
Project manager: Russell Porter
Production: Jess Brisley

A CIP catalogue record for this book is available from the British Library

Printed in Dubai

10 9 8 7 6 5 4 3 2 1

THE LITTLE BOOK OF
IRISH
BLESSINGS

MAY YOUR DAYS BE MANY
AND YOUR TROUBLES BE FEW

CONTENTS

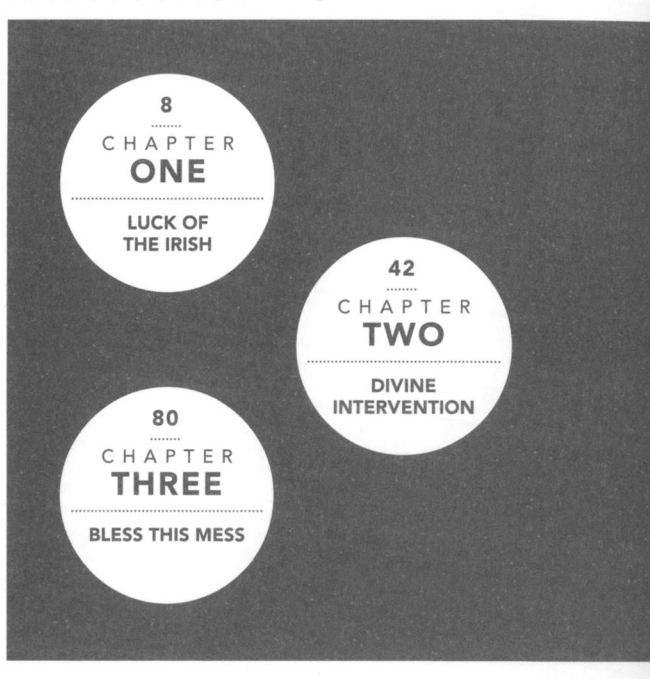

INTRODUCTION

When it comes to being blessed, Ireland is the place we all know best. A nation pouring with poetry, mythology and majesty (and whiskey), and a wealth of iconic ancient traditions. A land full of ire, for sure, and troubles, of course, but a place where citizens are free to voice passions 'til hoarse. Yes, I'm sure you'll agree, Ireland requires little introduction from me.

Famed for its poets and playwrights, Ireland is a realm where every written and spoken word packs the punch of a verb, each one as necessary as that last drop of Guinness. From Wilde to Joyce, Beckett or Binchy, Heaney to Shaw, and many, many more, this emerald isle can confidently express itself from shore to shore.

And Irish blessings could not be more, well, Irish, in this respect.

As time-honoured as they are wise, and as important as they are profound, Irish blessings are ideal for all types of occasions – from good luck to good riddance, declarations of friendship to congratulatory toasts,

proclamations of spiritual faith and secular hope,
to simple wishful thinking and basic expressions of
compassion.

Over the last 5,000 years, give or take, Irish
blessings have evolved into Christian interpretations
from Celtic folk and druidic traditions – but they've always
been unique to Ireland. The nation's patron saint, Patrick,
was perhaps even one of the earliest enthusiasts for Irish
Blessings to merge the old with the new with his now
beloved prayer (see page 160). And it's his love of Ireland
that we're all here to celebrate.

This *Little Guide to Irish Blessings* is a tiny tome for
your home, a perfect little pick-me-up complete with all
the wonderful wit and wisdom you've not only come to
expect from the Irish but also may desperately need to
rehydrate your mind, body and soul after one too many
St Patrick's Day toasts.

So, Happy St Patrick's Day to you and, never forget…
Éirinn go Brách!

chapter
ONE

LUCK OF THE IRISH

It's no coincidence that the Irish are considered the luckiest of all – they not only have the most beautiful land in the world, they also have the luck of a shamrock guiding them (especially a four-leafed one), a clover blessed by St Patrick himself as the symbol of the Holy Trinity.

However, should you know someone who requires backup support for good fortune this St Patrick's Day, these blessings are guaranteed to help them strike it even luckier...

If you're lucky enough to be Irish... you're lucky enough.

Irish proverb

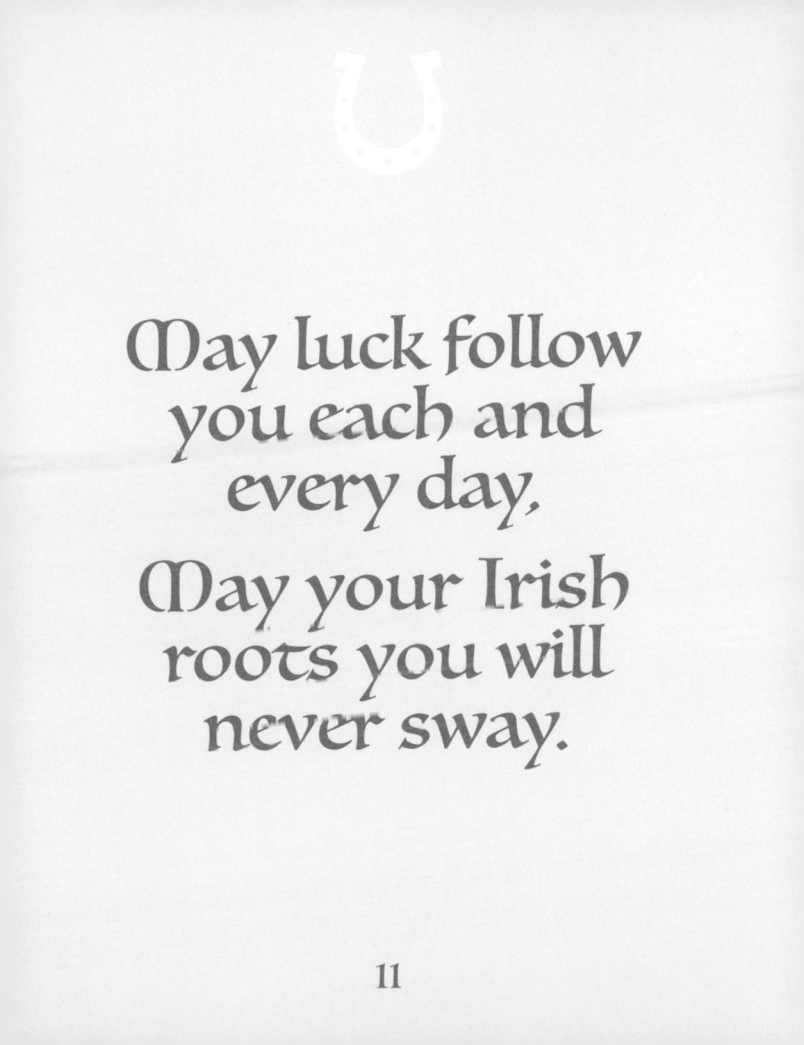

May luck follow
you each and
every day,

May your Irish
roots you will
never sway.

May the leprechauns
be near you,

To spread luck along
your way.

And may all the Irish angels,

Smile upon you
on St Patrick's Day.

May there be rain at your funeral.*

* A sign of good luck!

Wishing you a rainbow for
    sunlight after showers,
Miles and miles of Irish smiles
For golden happy hours,
Shamrocks at your doorway
For luck and laughter too,
And a host of friends that
    never ends
Each day your whole life through!

May the luck of the
Irish possess you.

May the devil fly off
with your worries.

May God bless you
forever and ever.

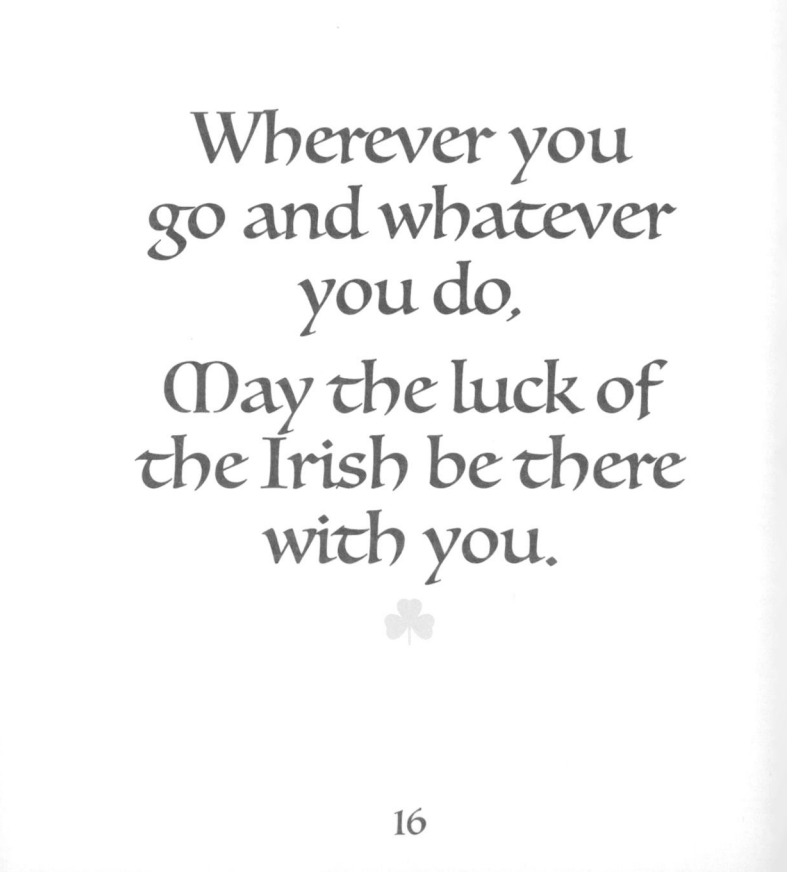

Wherever you
go and whatever
you do,

May the luck of
the Irish be there
with you.

May you have all the
happiness and luck that
life can hold,

And at the end of all your
rainbows may you find a
pot of gold.

May your pockets
be heavy and your heart
be light,

May good luck pursue
you each morning
and night.

May the luck of the Irish,
Lead to happiest heights.
And the highway you travel,
Be lined with green lights.

May luck be
a friend to ye,

And be with ye in
all yer days,

And may trouble
be to ye,

A stranger, always.

May luck be your
friend in whatever
you do and may
trouble be always a
stranger to you.

May the Irish hills caress you,

May her lakes and rivers bless you.

May the luck of the Irish
enfold you.

May the blessings of Saint Patrick
behold you.

Lucky stars above you,
Sunshine on your way.
Many friends to love you,
Joy in work and play.
Laughter to outweigh each care,
In your heart a song.
And gladness waiting everywhere,
All your whole life long.

For each petal on
the shamrock,

This brings a wish your way.

Good health, good luck,
and happiness,

For today and every day.

Like the warmth
of the sun and the
light of the day,

May the luck
of the Irish
shine bright on
your way.

Gold coins in the river,
or a four-leaf clover,

May your luck
on this day give you hope
it is not over.

🍀

To wish you the luck o' the Irish, begorra!

Not just for today but for every tomorra,

May you seize every chance,

To kick back and dance!

May God send
you good fortune,
contentment
and peace,

And may all your
blessings forever
increase.

An Irish wish from the
heart of a friend,

May good fortune always
be yours,

And may your joys
never end.

May you be poor in misfortune,
Rich in blessings,
Slow to make enemies,
Quick to make friends,
But rich or poor, quick or slow,
May you know nothing but
happiness from this day forward.

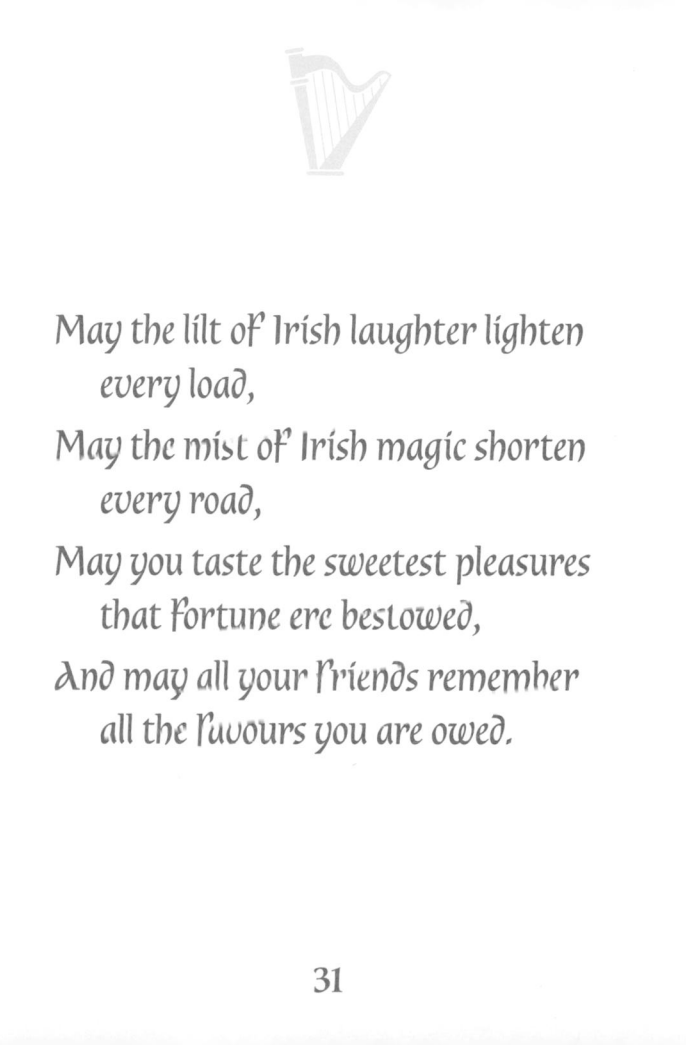

May the lilt of Irish laughter lighten
  every load,

May the mist of Irish magic shorten
  every road,

May you taste the sweetest pleasures
  that fortune ere bestowed,

And may all your friends remember
  all the favours you are owed.

May misfortune
follow you the rest of
your life... and never
catch up!

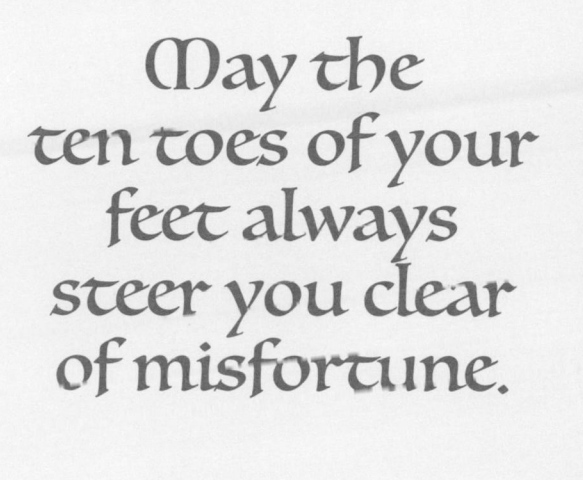

May the
ten toes of your
feet always
steer you clear
of misfortune.

May the blessed
sunlight shine
on you and warm
your heart,
Till it glows like a
great peat fire.

May strong arms hold you,
Caring hearts tend you,
And may love await you
at every step.

May you live to comb
the hair of your children's
children.

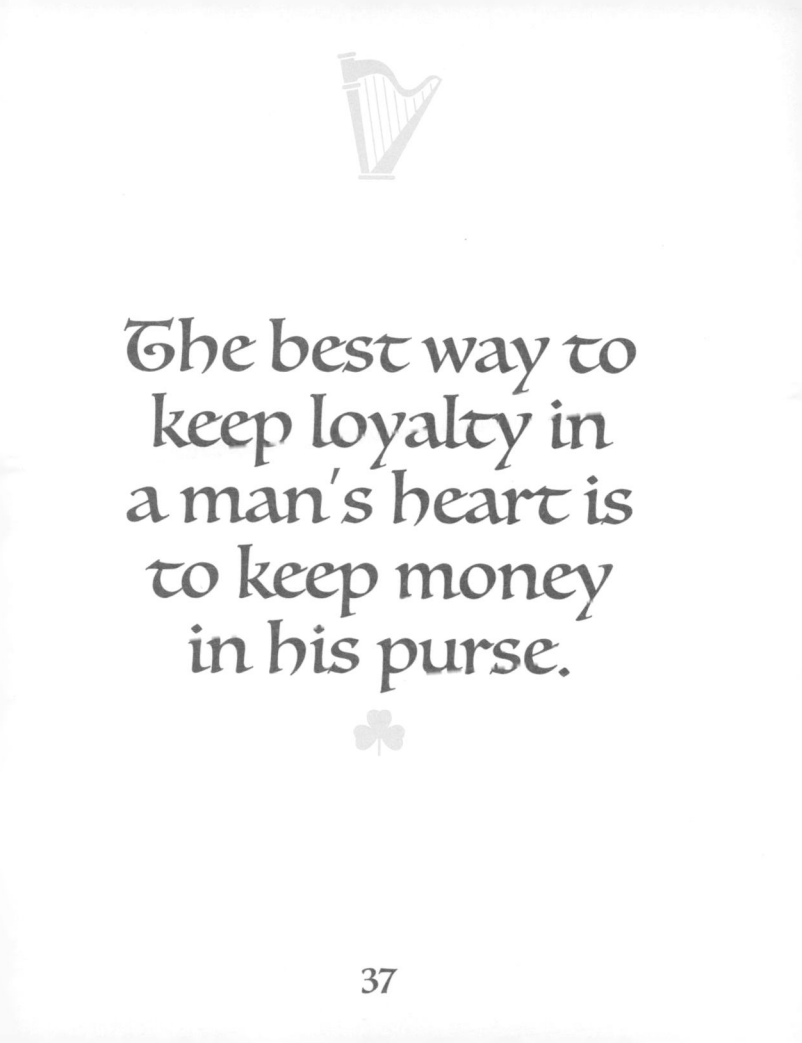

The best way to
keep loyalty in
a man's heart is
to keep money
in his purse.

May the face of every
good news,

And the back of every
bad news,

Be toward us.

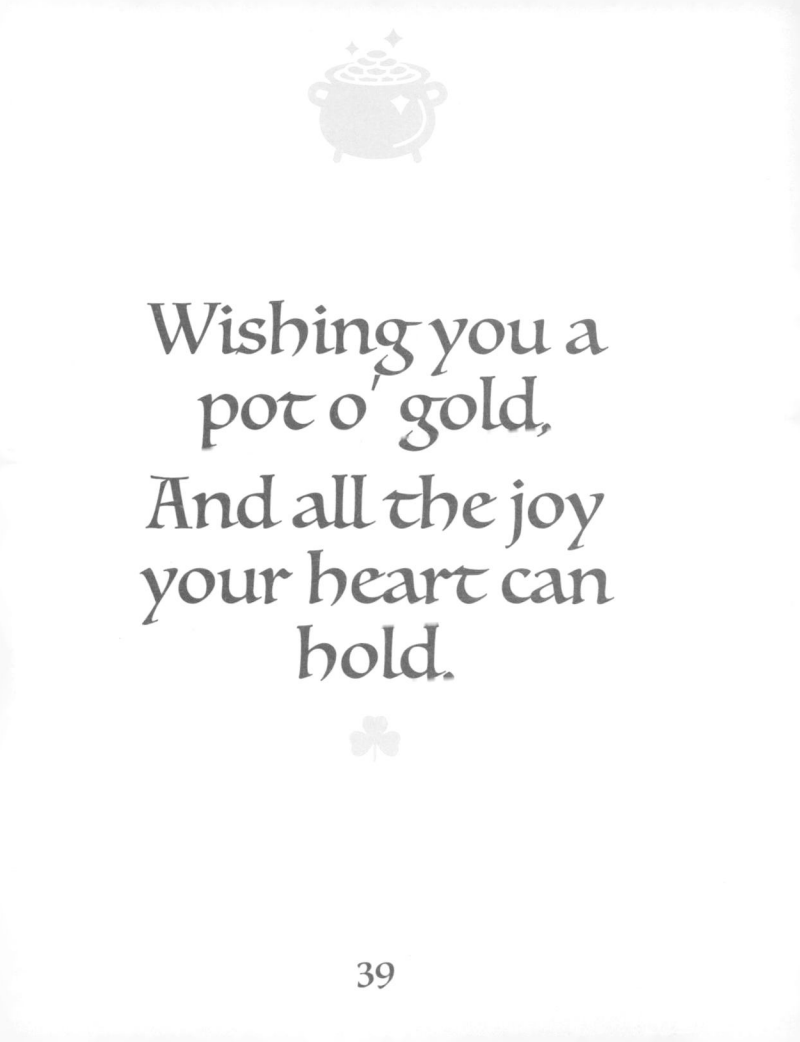

Wishing you a
pot o' gold,

And all the joy
your heart can
hold.

May the
enemies of
Ireland
never meet
a friend.

May the blessings
of each day,

Be the blessings you
need most.

CHAPTER
TWO

DIVINE INTERVENTION

Irish blessings have evolved to suit the needs
of the citizens of Ireland, transforming
from Celtic folk traditions of ancient times
into everyday desires for divine intervention, in
whatever form it wishes to take.

The positive blessings revealed within are a
godsend for those looking up at a higher power
to answer their prayer...

Here's to those
who wish us well,
As for the rest,
they can go to Hell!

Like the gold of the sun,
Like the light of the day May,
God's love and protection,
Shine bright on your way.

I said an Irish prayer today,

Especially for you.

For family, true friends,

And faith to last your whole life through.

I asked the Lord to give you,

A shelter from the storm.

And just enough of His good grace to keep
you safe and warm.

I prayed the road would rise to meet you, all
along your way,

And smilin' Irish eyes would greet you every
single day.

May God give you,
For every storm, a rainbow,
For every fear, a smile,
For every care, a promise
And a blessing in each trial.
For every problem life sends,
A faithful friend to share.
For every sigh, a sweet song,
And an answer for each prayer.

May the road rise to meet you.

May the wind be always at your back.

May the sunshine warm upon
    your face.

And rains fall soft upon your fields.

And until we meet again, may God
    hold you in the hollow of His hand.

May those who love us, love us,

And those that don't, may God turn
   their hearts.

And if He doesn't turn their hearts,

May He turn their ankles, so we'll
   know them by their limping. *

More of a cure than a blessing!

49

God bless the corners of this house,
And be the lintel blest.
And bless the hearth,
And bless the board,
And bless each place of rest.
Bless each door that opens wide,
To stranger as to kin,
And bless each crystal windowpane,
That lets the sunshine in.
And bless the rooftree overhead,
And every sturdy wall,
The peace of man, the peace of God,
The peace of love on all.

God bless our Irish
home,

With mercy from above,

And may he grace this
humble place,

With heaven's peace
and love.

Bless this house O Lord we pray,
Keep it safe by night and day.
Bless these walls so firm and stout,
Keeping want and trouble out.
Bless the roof and chimney tall,
Let thy peace be over all.
Bless these windows shining bright,
Letting in God's heavenly light.
Bless the folk who dwell within,
Keeping them pure and free from sin.
Bless us all that we may be fit,
O Lord, to dwell with thee.

May joy and peace
surround you both,
contentment latch your
door, and happiness
be with you now and God
bless you ever more.

Bless the four corners of
    this house.

Bless the hearth, kitchen and
    place of rest.

Bless the door that opens
    wide to stranger and to kin.

Bless the windows and roof
    overhead.

Pray God's blessing that we
    are always fed.

May the grace
of God's love
abide within our
home and within
our hearts.

May your days be many and your
troubles be few,

May all God's blessings descend
upon you.

May peace be within you, may
your heart be strong,

May you find what you're seeking
wherever you roam.

May you have:

A world of wishes at
your command,

God and his angels close
to hand.

Friends and family, their love
impart,

And Irish blessings in
your heart.

May you have love
that never ends,

Lots of money, and
lots of friends.

Health be yours,
whatever you do,

And may God send
many blessings to you!

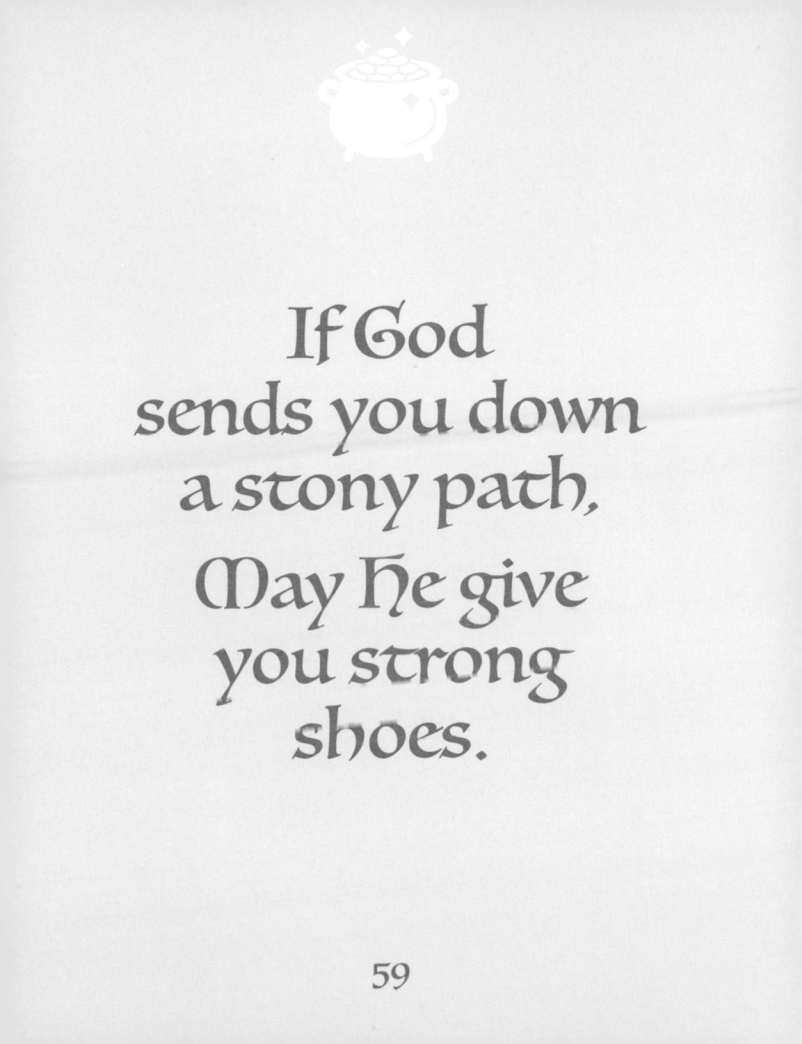

If God
sends you down
a stony path,

May He give
you strong
shoes.

May the grace of
God's protection,

And His great
love abide.

Within your home and
within the hearts,

Of all who dwell inside.

May there always be work for your
hands to do,

May your purse always hold a coin or
two.

May the sun always shine warm on
your windowpane,

May a rainbow be certain to follow
each rain.

May the hand of a friend always be
near you,

And may God fill your heart with
gladness to cheer you.

God bless you now and always with the gift of Irish cheer.

God give to you a happy heart and keep you through the year.

When I count
my blessings,
I count you
twice.

May God
bless you.

May the raindrops fall lightly
    on your brow,
May the soft winds freshen
    your spirit.
May the sunshine brighten
    your heart,
May the burdens of the day
    rest lightly upon you.
And may God enfold you in
    the mantle of His love.

May the good earth be soft under you
    when you rest upon it,

And may it rest easy over you when,
    at the last, you lay out under it,

And may it rest so lightly over you
    that your soul may be out from
    under it quickly, and up, and off,

And be on its way to God.

May God grant
you many years to live,

For sure he must
be knowing.

The Earth has angels
all too few.

And Heaven
is overflowing.

🍀

May your Irish pride be strong,
But may you admit it when
    you're wrong.
God needed laughter in the world,
So he made the Irish race.
For they can meet life with a smile,
And turn a huppy face.

May you be blessed always with,
A sunbeam to warm you,
A moonbeam to charm you,
A sheltering angel,
So nothing can harm you.
Laughter to cheer you,
Faithful friends near you,
And whenever you pray,
Heaven to hear you.

Wee little one, may
you always walk in
sunshine, may you
never want for more.

May Irish angels rest
their wings beside your
nursery door.

May music flow through your
    spirit like the River Shannon.

May your body be as strong and
    upright as the Rock of Cashel.

May the grace of swans move your
    feet lightly,

And may the angels in Heaven

Lift you to great heights always.

O Lord, bless this child as it sleeps,
    we pray, and hold it close to
    you each day.
Let angels stand guard until it's
    time to rise and softly sing
    Irish lullabies.
Bless the roof and chimney tall,
    let thy peace be over all.

These things, I warmly
wish for you,

Someone to love, some
work to do,

A bit of o' sun, a bit o' cheer.

And a guardian angel
always near.

🍀

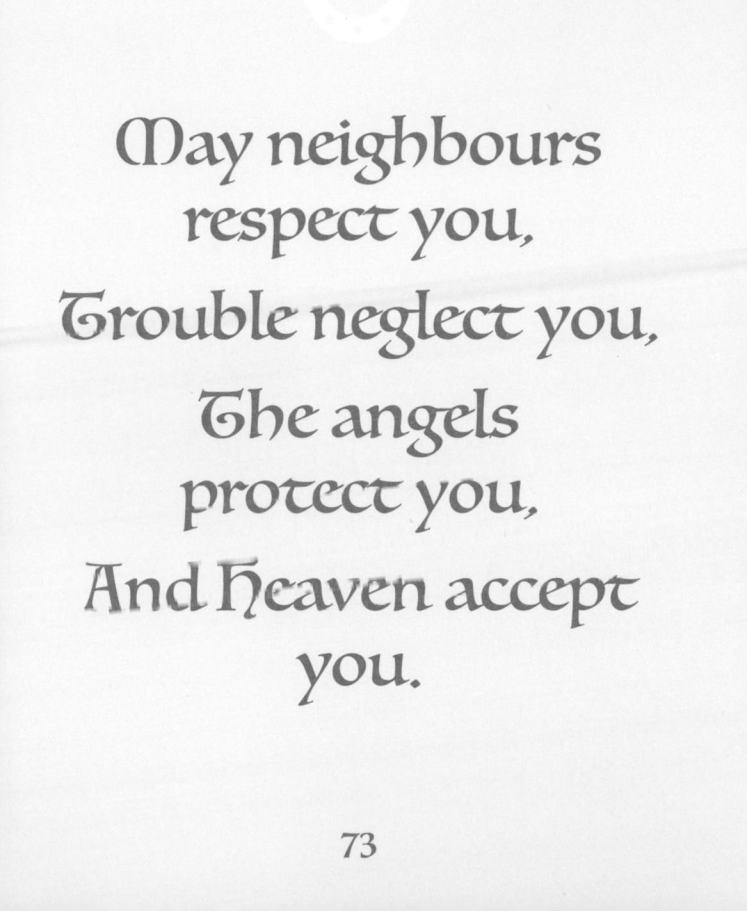

May neighbours
respect you,

Trouble neglect you,

The angels
protect you,

And Heaven accept
you.

73

Ample food and sturdy drink,
a clean pillow for your head.

And may you be forty years
in heaven before the devil
knows you're dead!

May the
cat eat you
and
the devil eat
the cat.

May the good
Lord take a liking
to you...

But not too
soon!

May these walls be filled with
    laughter,
May it reach from floor to rafter.
May the roof keep out the rain,
May sunshine warm each
    windowpane.
And may the door be open wide,
To let the good Lord's love inside.

May the Lord keep
you in his hand but
never close his fist tight
on you.

May you live a long life
full of gladness and
health, with a pocket full
of gold as the least of
your wealth.

CHAPTER
THREE

BLESS THIS MESS

The 21st-century world is in a bit of a pickle, isn't it? Nothing seems to be getting any better.

Thankfully, the blessings that unfold here are precisely the snack-sized bites of salvation you've been searching for, those bright-light blessings that glow in the dark, perfect to employ on those rainy days when you need them the most.

A hundred thousand welcomes
when you enter...

A hundred thousand memories
when you leave...

A hundred thousand angels
with you always.

** From the traditional Irish blessing Céad Mile Fáilte,
which means "A Hundred Thousand Welcomes".*

May the blessings of light
    be upon you,
Light without and light within.
And in all your comings and
    goings,
May you ever have a kindly
    greeting,
From them you meet along
    the road.

When the first light
of sun – Bless you.

When the long day is
done – Bless you.

In your smiles and your
tears – Bless you.

Through each day
of your years –
Bless you.

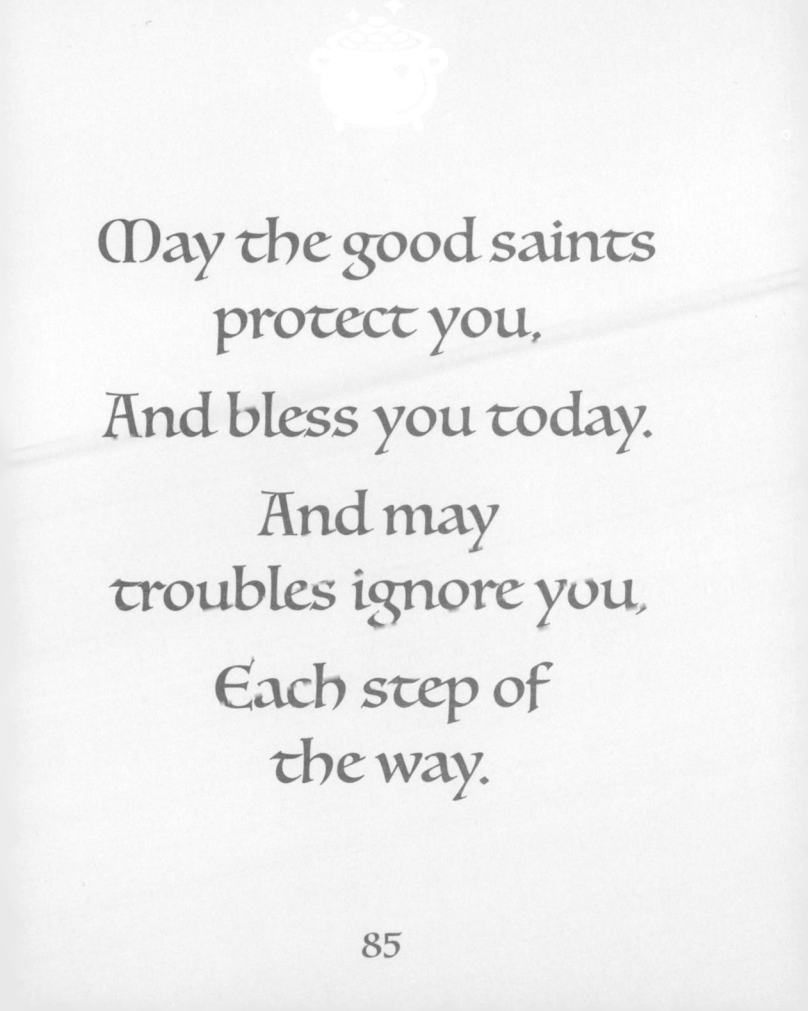

May the good saints
protect you,

And bless you today.

And may
troubles ignore you,

Each step of
the way.

May your adventures
all be fun,

May they be full of
flowers and sun.

May the roads you
venture down,

Find blessings that surround.

Always remember
to forget,

The troubles that passed
away.

But never forget to
remember,

The blessings that come
each day.

May you have the health to wear it. *

A blessing for someone when they receive a new item of clothing.

More power
to your elbow. *

* A blessing meaning "Well done".

May the most
you wish for
be the least
you get.

Good land, good harvest, good
  roof above,
Good friends, good gab,
Good helping of love,
Good hearts in good prayer to
  the good
Lord upraised...
For this we give thanks, good
  saints be praised.

May love and laughter light your days
    and warm your heart and home,

May good and faithful friends be yours
    wherever you may roam,

May peace and plenty bless your world
    with joy that long endures,

May all life's passing seasons,

Bring the best to you and yours.

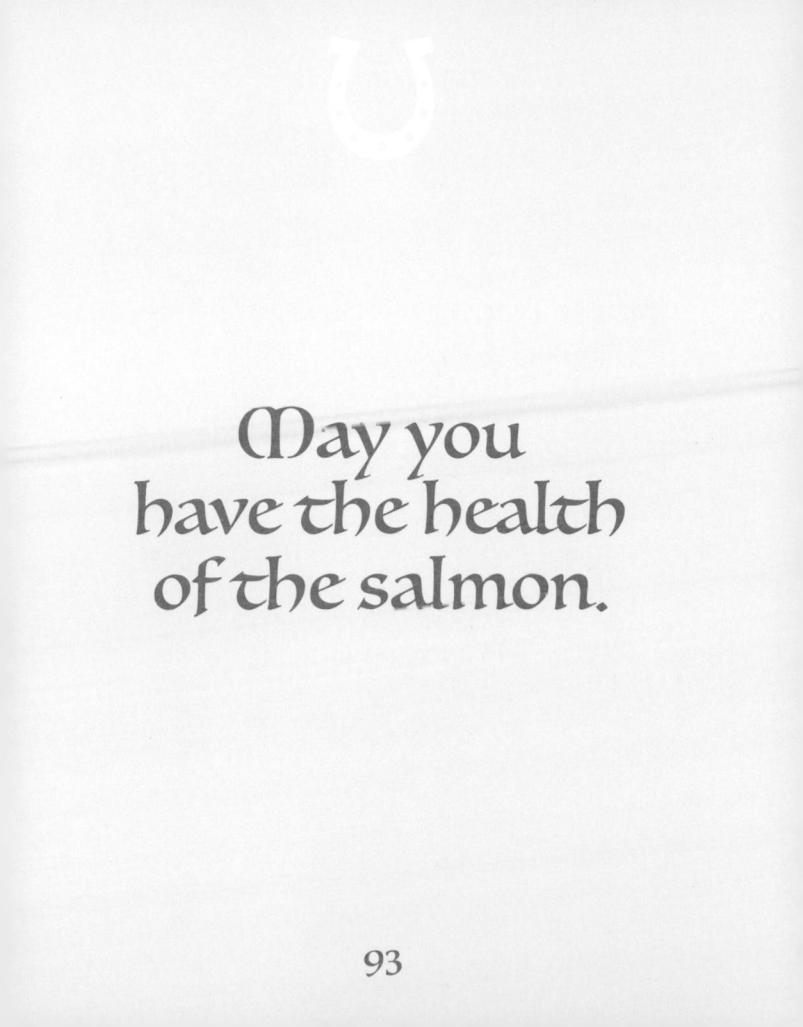

May you
have the health
of the salmon.

May your mornings bring joy, and your
    evenings bring peace,

May your troubles grow few as your
    blessings increase.

May the happiest day of your future be no
    worse than the happiest of your past,

May your hands be forever clasped in
    friendship and your love always last.

May peace and plenty
bless your home with
joy that long endures,

And may life's passing
seasons bring the best
to you and yours.

May your blessings
outnumber the
shamrocks that grow,

And may trouble avoid
you wherever you go.

Leave the table hungry.

Leave the bed sleepy.

Leave the tavern thirsty.

A traditional Irish blessing for a long, happy life.

Bless you when the first
light of sun,

Bless you when the long
day is done.

Bless you in your smiles
and your tears,

Bless you through each day
of your years.

St Brigid's Prayer

May Brigid bless the house
wherein you dwell.

Bless every fireside, every wall
and door.

Bless every heart that beats
beneath its roof.

Bless every hand that toils to
bring it joy.

Bless every foot that walks its
portals through.

May Brigid bless the house that
shelters you.

Bless you and yours,

As well as the cottage
you live in.

May the roof overhead
be well-thatched,

And those inside be
well-matched.

May your
troubles be less,

And your
blessings be more.

And nothing but
happiness,

Come through
your door.

Bless your little Irish heart and every other Irish part.

Peace on your
hand and
health to all who
shake it.

May you live
as long as you
want, and never
want as long as
you live.

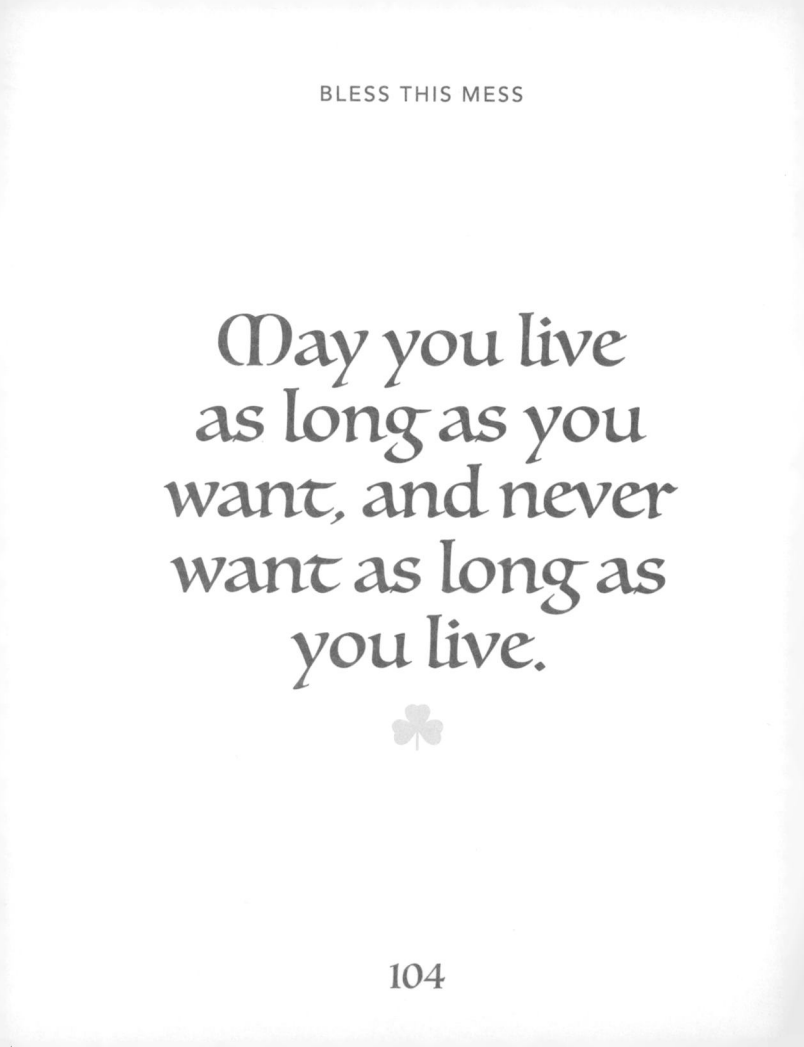

Here's to the grey goose,
With the golden wing.
A free country,
And a Fenian King.

Always remember
to forget,

The things that made
you sad.

But never forget to
remember,

The things that made
you glad.

I wish thee health,
I wish thee wealth,
I wish thee golden store,
And after death I wish thee
    Heaven,
And who could wish thee more.

May your feet never sweat,
your neighbour gives you
ne're a treat.

When flowers bloom,
I hope you'll not sneeze,

and may you always have
someone to squeeze!

May the
leprechauns
dance
over your bed
and bring you
sweet dreams.

Happiness being a dessert so sweet,

May life give you more than you can ever eat.

As you slide down the
banister of life,

May the splinters never point
the wrong way.

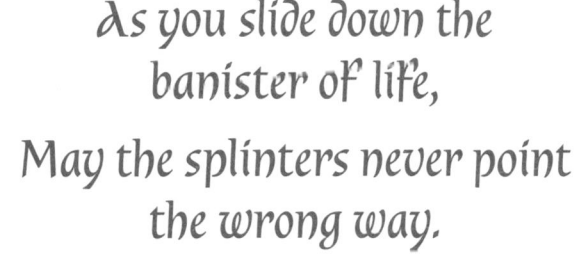

May the roof of your house never fall in,

And those beneath it never fall out.

May your home
always be too
small to hold all
your friends.

May green be the grass you
  walk on,

May blue be the sky above you,

May pure be the joys that
  surround you.

May true be the hearts that
  love you.

May you live long,
Die happy,
And rate a mansion
in heaven.

When the roaring
flames of your love
have burned down
to embers,

May you find that
you've married your
best friend.

May you always find three
welcomes in life:

In a garden during summer,

At a hearth during winter,

And in the hearts of friends
throughout all your years.

Here's to a fellow
who smiles,

When life runs along
like a song.

And here's to the lad
who can smile

When everything goes
dead wrong.

May brooks and trees
and singing hills,

Join in the chorus, too.

And every gentle wind
that blows,

Send happiness to you.

119

chapter
FOUR

EMERALD ISLE

The more Irish the blessing, the better—
that's what my Irish grandmother always
used to say as she'd deliver a belter of a
blessing before breakfast.

And the blessings in this chapter are
proper polished gems! But, be warned,
don't rub them all at once or you'll
wear them out.

Ten Commandments for the Irish

Thou shalt be loyal to family, friends
and faith.

Thou shalt keep thy Irish eyes a-smilin.

Thou shalt shy away from blarney.

Thou shalt honour thy motherland.

Thou shalt see the Trinity in every shamrock.

Thou shalt halve each potato out of love.

Thou shalt be kind to wee ones everywhere.

Thou shalt be generous with blessings, song
and stories.

Thou shalt follow every rainbow.

Thou shalt rest easy in the hollow of
God's hand.

May your home be filled
with laughter,

May your pockets be filled
with gold,

And may you have all the
happiness,

Your Irish heart can hold.

May your heart be
warm and happy,

With the lilt of Irish
laughter.

Every day in every way,

And forever and
ever after.

May the embers from
the open hearth warm
your hands,

May the sun's rays from the
Irish sky warm your face,

May the children's bright
smiles warm your heart,

May the everlasting love
I give you warm your soul.

Health and long life to you,

Land without rent to you,

A child every year to you,

If you can't go to Heaven,

May you die in Ireland.

Here's wishing you the top o' life
without a single tumble.

Here's wishing you the smiles o' life
and not a single grumble.

Here's wishing you the best o' life
and not a claw about it.

Here's wishing you the joy in life
and not a day without it.

May those who
love bring love
back to you,

And may all the
wishes you wish
come true!

I-rish you a very nice
place to live,

I-rish God's greatest
gifts he'll give.

I-rish you health, and wealth,
and more

I-rish your smilin' face
were at my door!

May you never
be bored,

May through life
you will soar.

May adventures
allow you to fly,

And have successes
that are high.

May you realize
how special you are,
May you see yourself
as we do, a star.

May there be
just enough clouds
in your life
to create a glorious
sunset.

May there be a
generation of children,

On the children of
your children.

May there be better legs
under your table before
the new crop is up.

May your hair
never fall out
and your beard
ever be bushy.

May your heart be light
and happy,

May your smile be
big and wide,

And may your pockets
always have,

A coin or two inside!

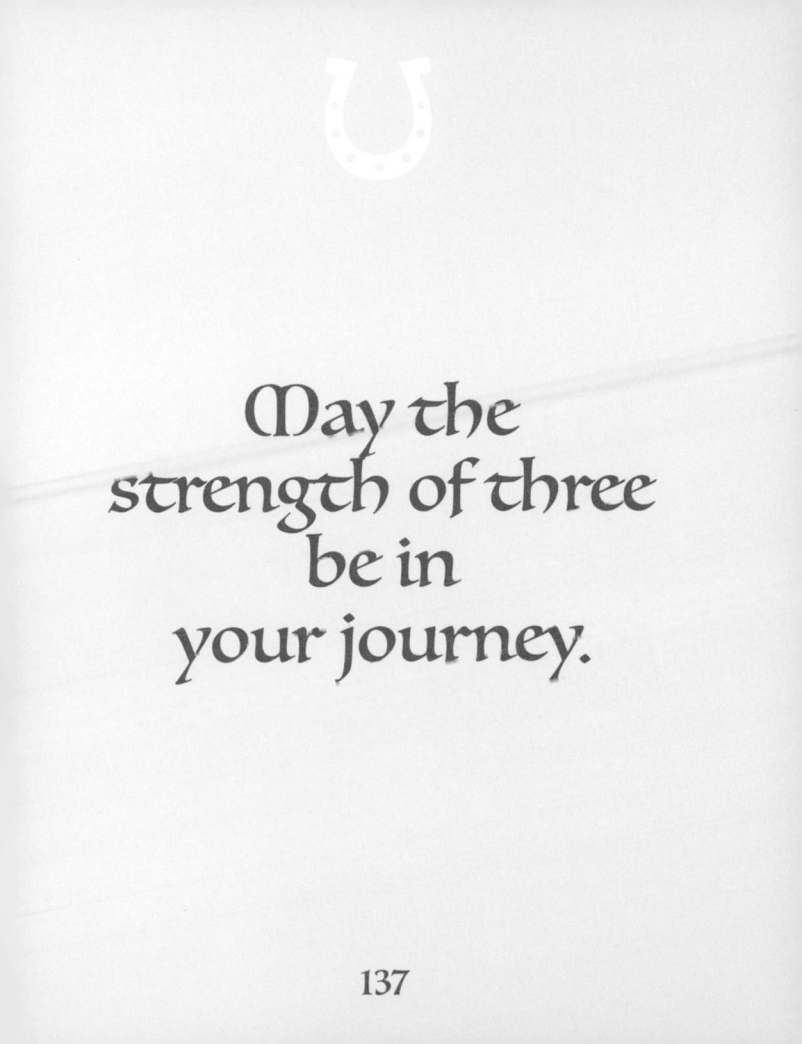

May the
strength of three
be in
your journey.

May the grass grow
long on the road to Hell for
want of use.

May the dreams you
hold dearest,

Be those which come true.

The kindness you spread,

Keep returning to you.

May all your troubles
be little ones
and all your little ones
be trouble free.

*May the hinges
of our friendship never
grow rusty!*

🍀

Here's to eyes in
your heads and none in
your spuds.

May your
troubles be as few
and as far apart
as my
grandmother's
teeth.

To all the days here
and after,

May they be filled
with fond memories,
happiness and laughter.

May the rains sweep gently
across your fields,

May the sun warm the land,

May every good seed you have
planted bear fruit

And may late summer
find you standing in fields
of plenty.

May you have the
hindsight to know
where you've been, the
foresight to know
where you're going…
and the insight to know
when you've gone
too far.

May the best day
of your past
be the worst day of
your future.

Let your heart be glad
for the harvest done,

And may your winter
be warm the whole
season long.

For the test of the heart
is trouble,

And it always comes
with years.

And the smile that is worth
the praises of earth,

Is the smile that shines
through the tears.

149

May you get
all your wishes but one,

So you always have
something to strive for.

May peace and plenty
be the first,

To lift the latch to your door.

And happiness be your guest
today and evermore.

May the friendships you make,

Be those which endure,

And all of your grey clouds,

Be small ones for sure.

And trusting in Him,

To whom we all pray,

May a song fill your heart,

Every step of the way.

May you live
all the days of
your life.

May you always have walls for
  the winds,
A roof for the rain,
Tea beside the fire,
Laughter to cheer you,
Those you love near you,
And all your heart might desire.

May your thoughts be as glad
as the shamrocks,

May your heart be as light
as a song.

May each day bring you bright
happy hours,

That stay with you all
year long.

155

May you have warm words
on a cold evening,

A full moon on a dark night,

And the road downhill all
the way to your door.

When times are hard may
hardness never turn your
heart to stone.

May you always remember
when the shadows fall you
do not walk alone.

chapter
FIVE

SAINTS AND SLÁINTE!

St Patrick's Day is celebrated around the world every March 17. It's a day for Irish people, and their friends, to count their blessings together.

For this final chapter, we've compiled the perfect toasts and blessings to celebrate your good health and luck this St Patrick's Day.

All together now: SLÁINTE!

St Patrick's Prayer

May your days be many, and your troubles
be few.

May all God's blessings descend upon you.

May peace be within you, may your heart
be strong.

May you find what you're seeking wherever
you roam.

May the strength of God pilot us, may the
wisdom of God instruct us.

May the hand of God protect us, may the
word of God direct us.

May thy salvation, O Lord, be always ours
this day and for evermore.

Amen.

May you receive
mercy and grace, death
without sin and may the
righteous gone before
you receive their share
of eternal glory.

May you have
a healthy heart
and a
wet mouth!

May you have rye bread
to do you good,

Wheaten bread to sweeten
your blood,

Barley bread to do you
no harm,

And oatmeal bread
to strengthen your arm.

May you never
bear the heavy
load of an empty
stomach.

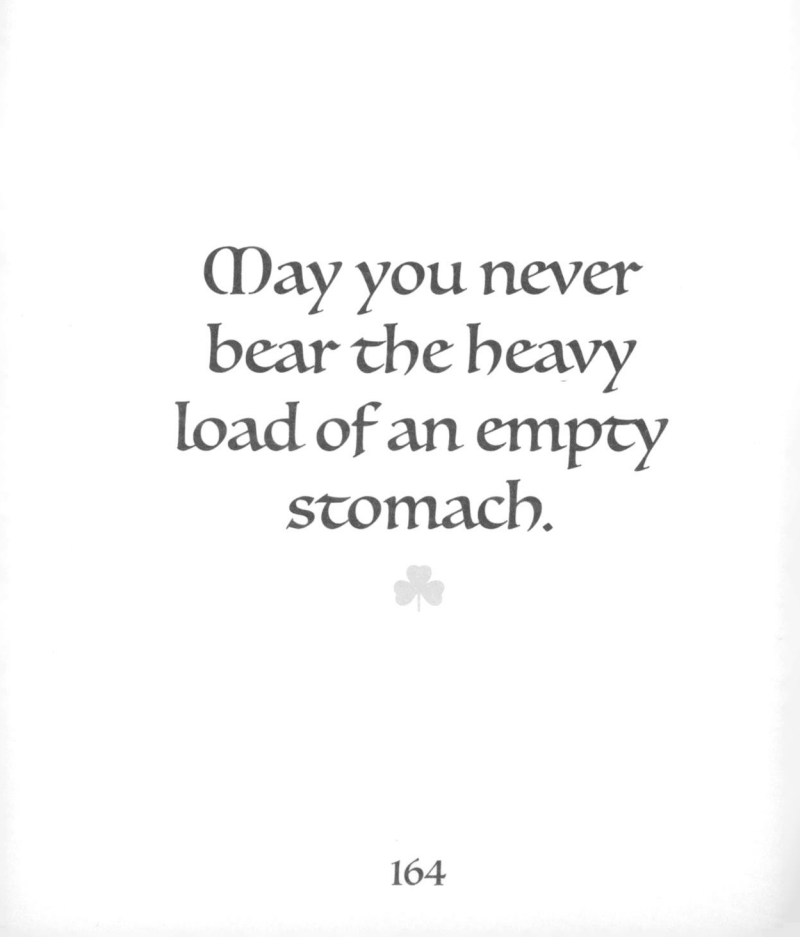

May you grow old
in the face,

Be treasured and cared
for with grace.

May big headaches
and little fevers
be always
far from you.

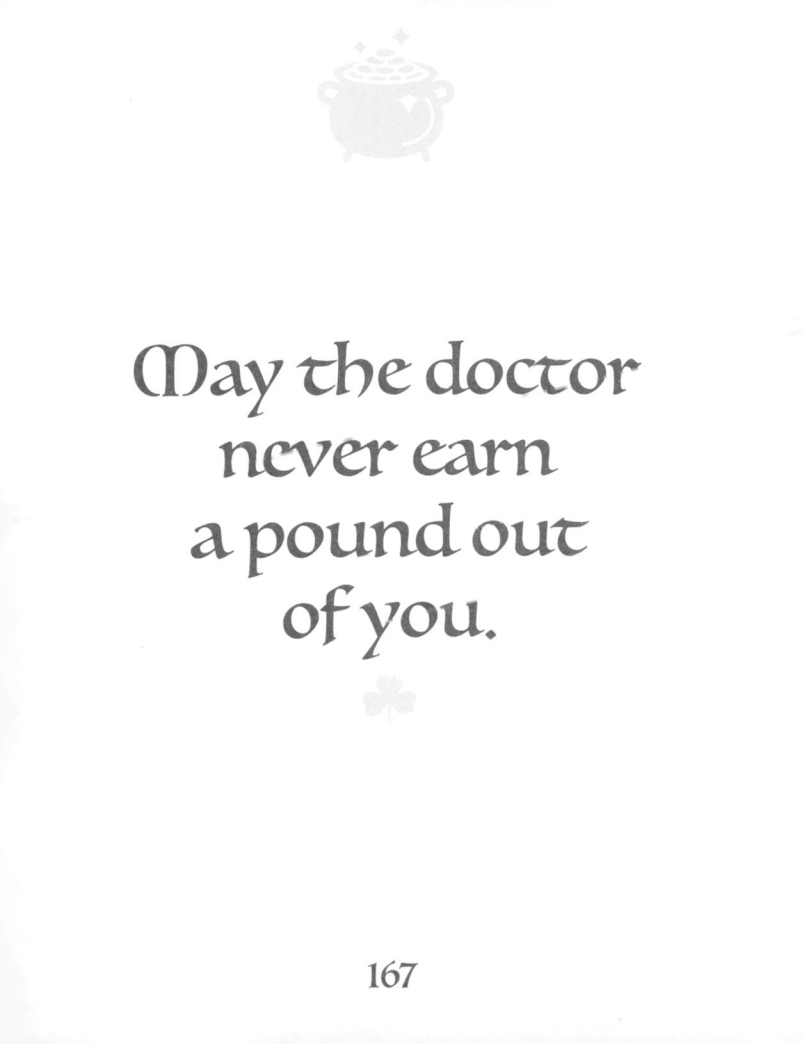

May the doctor
never earn
a pound out
of you.

May I see you grey,
And combing your
grandchildren's hair.

🍀

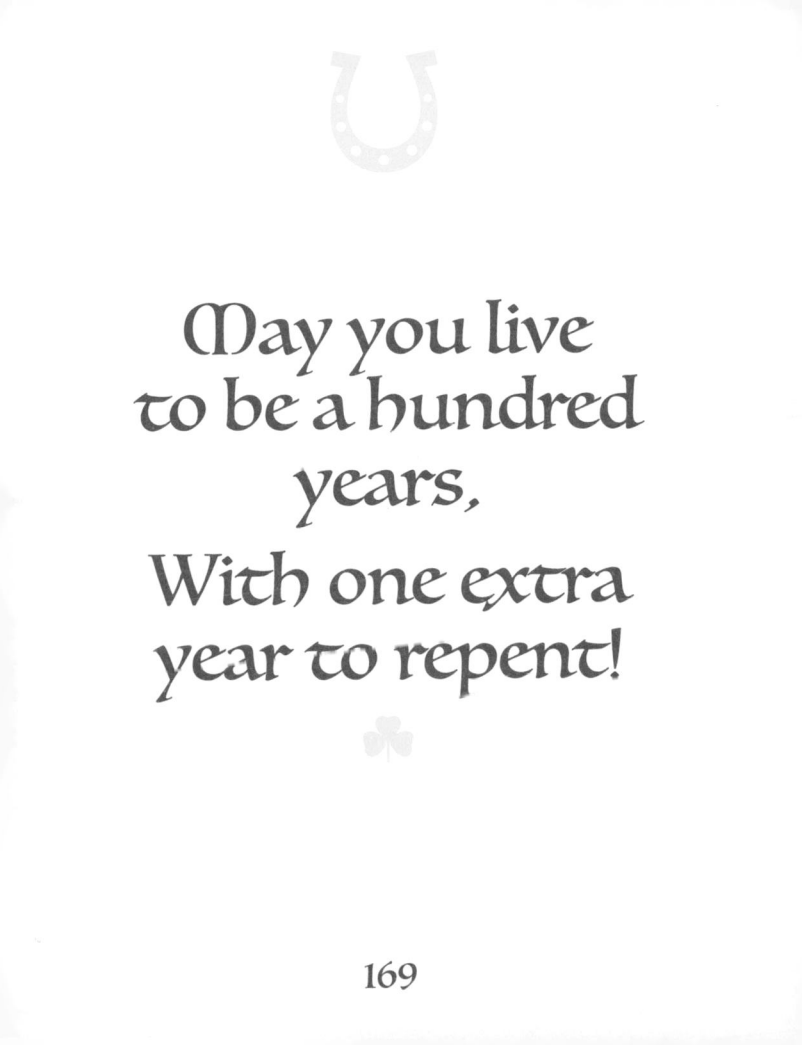

May you live
to be a hundred
years,
With one extra
year to repent!

We drink to your coffin. May it be built from the wood of a hundred-year-old oak tree that I shall plant tomorrow.

Peace to friends,
and peace
to kin, peace to
this home
and the
family within.

May soft be the grass you
  walk on,
May fair be the skies above
  you,
May true be the joys that
  surround you,
May dear be the hearts
  that love you.

Come in the evening,
Come in the morning,
Come when expected,
Come without warning,
Thousands of welcomes,
You'll find here before you,
And the oftener you come,
The more we'll adore you.

My friends are the
best friends,

Loyal, willing and able.

Now let's get to drinking!

All glasses off the table!

Irish toast

May you always
have a clean shirt, a clear
conscience,

And enough coins
in your pocket to buy a pint!

May you die in
bed at 95,

Shot by a
jealous spouse.

May your right hand
always be stretched out
in friendship,

But never in want.

May the frost
never afflict our spuds,

May the leaves of
your cabbage always be free
from worms,

May the crows
never pick your haystack,

And may your donkey
always be in foal.

May you never forget,

What is worth
remembering.

Or remember what is,

Best forgotten.

Here's to the
health of
your enemies'
enemies.

Here's health and prosperity,

To you and all your posterity,

And them that doesn't drink
with sincerity,

That they be damned for
all eternity.

Here's to you and yours,

And to mine and ours.

And if mine and ours,

Ever come across to you and yours,

I hope you and yours will do,

As much for mine and ours,

As mine and ours have done,

For you and yours!

Irish toast

May the winds of
fortune sail you, may
you sail a gentle sea,

And may it always be
the other guy who says
this drink's on me.

I drink to your health
when I'm with you,

I drink to your health
when I'm alone,

I drink to your health
so often,

I'm starting to worry
about my own.

Here's to a long life and a
  merry one.

A quick death and an easy one.

A pretty girl and an honest one.

A cold beer and another one!

Irish toast

May the love and
protection Saint Patrick
can give,

Be yours in abundance,

As long as you live.

🍀

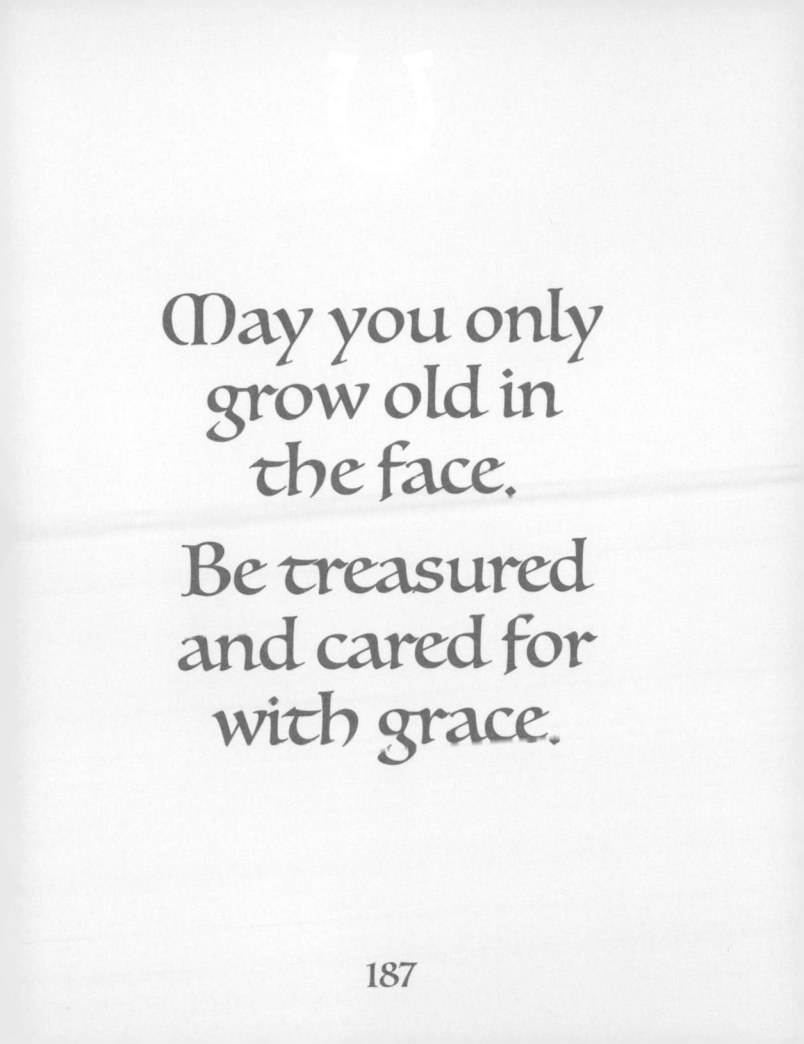

May you only
grow old in
the face.

Be treasured
and cared for
with grace.

Here's to me, and here's to you. And here's to love and laughter.

I'll be true as long as you. And not one moment after.

Irish toast

May the joys of today,
Be those of tomorrow.
The goblets of life,
Hold no dregs of
sorrow.

Here's to you
and here's to me,
I pray that friends
we'll always be,
but if by chance we
disagree, the heck
with you and here's
to me.

Irish toast

Here's to our wives,
And here's
to our sweethearts,
May the two
never meet!

Irish toast

Here's to the land of the shamrock so green,

Here's to each lad and his darlin' Colleen,

Here's to the ones we love dearest and most.

May God bless old Ireland, that's this Irishman's toast!

Irish toast